D0358684

MA.

/11 OE

- 1

1 9

Get Cooking!

DK

DK

LONDON, NEW YORK, MUNICH,
MELBOURNE, and DELHI

Senior editor Carrie Love
Senior art editor Gemma Fletcher
Designer Lauren Rosier

Photographer Dave King
Home economist Kate Blinman
Science consultant Donald R Franceschetti
Production editor Siu Chan
Production controller Kara Wallace
Jacket designer Gemma Fletcher
Publishing manager Bridget Giles
Creative director Jane Bull
Category publisher Mary Ling

First published in Great Britain in 2012 by
Dorling Kindersley Limited
80 Strand, London WC2R 0RL
Penguin Group (UK)

10 9 8 7 6 5 4 3 2 1
001-182774-02/12

Copyright © 2012 Dorling Kindersley
Limited

All rights reserved. No part of this
publication may be reproduced, stored in
a retrieval system, or transmitted in any
form or by any means, electronic,
mechanical, photocopying, recording, or
otherwise, without the prior written
permission of the copyright owner.

A CIP catalogue record for this book
is available from the British Library.

ISBN: 978-1-40539-144-3

Printed and bound in China
by Hung Hing

Discover more at
www.dk.com

Contents

This is fun!

FLINTSHIRE
SIR Y FFLINT

C29 0000 0637 336

ASKEWS & HOLT	23-Oct-2012
J641.5	£7.99
MA	

Which one is your favourite recipe to make?

Introduction

Being able to cook is an important skill in life. It's a fun activity too. This book will inspire you and give you the confidence to try out new dishes for yourself, your family, and your friends.

You'll find simple recipes, such as how to boil an egg or bake muffins, to more complicated dishes, such as moussaka and meringues. Each recipe is clearly laid out and easy to follow.

Put your apron on and get cooking!

How this book works

It's important to carefully check the "You will need:" box before you go shopping for the ingredients.

Each recipe has an introduction to inspire and encourage you to try out the dish.

You'll find suggestions for alternative ingredients to try out or extra items of food to accompany a dish.

Keep an eye out for any "Special equipment:" you might need to complete a recipe. Make sure you have everything prepared before you get cooking.

Look out for me! I'm full of hints, tips, and interesting questions.

All the recipes contain steps in number order. You'll need to follow them in the right sequence or the recipe won't work.

Have you ever wondered why you need to knead dough, why you cry when you chop onions, and why chilli is such a spicy meal? Find out the scientific answers to these questions and more by reading the "Why???" boxes.

Getting started

Roll up your sleeves, wear an apron, tie up long hair, and wash your hands before you start any recipe. Store food correctly and follow expiry dates. Wash all fruit and vegetables before you use them in a recipe. Clean up any spillages as you go. Use separate chopping boards to cut up vegetables and meat. Wash your hands after handling raw meat and eggs.

KEY

Key to symbols used in the recipes:

 Check this symbol to find out how long it takes to prepare a recipe.

 This symbol tells you how long it takes to cook a dish.

 This symbol tells you how many servings a recipe makes. Bear in mind that really young children eat less so it would make more portions for younger children.

 This symbol means that a step requires closer adult supervision, or an adult should carry out the instructions. An adult should always be with a child when making any recipe from this book.

WEIGHTS AND MEASUREMENTS

Make sure you weigh out the ingredients correctly. Use measuring spoons, a measuring jug, and weighing scales where necessary. Measurements are written out in full below. You'll see the abbreviations in the "You will need:" boxes.

Metric measures:	Imperial measures:	Spoon measures:
g = grams	oz = ounces	tsp = teaspoon
ml = millilitres	lb = pounds	tbsp = tablespoon
	fl oz = fluid ounces	

A wooden spoon is a cook's friend. I'm used in lots of recipes.

Tools of the trade

It's important that you use the right equipment for each recipe. Most kitchens are equipped with the majority of these "tools". Remember to be careful around equipment that is sharp or uses electricity to power it. An adult should always supervise you while you're in the kitchen.

Peelers

Garlic crusher

Wooden spoons

Whisk

Basting brush

Kitchen scissors

Large spoon

Pizza cutter

Sharp Knife

Table Knife

Fork

Spoons

Grater

Baking trays

Loaf tin

Muffin tin

Pizza tray

Cutting boards

Small bowls

Large bowl

Colander

Glass bowls

Get the equipment ready before you start a recipe.

Food processor

Chopping board

Glass jar

Masher

Electric whisk

Spatula

Plastic spatula

Skewers

Measuring jug

Sieve

Food blender

Slotted spoon

Spaghetti claw

Did you know that the bottom of a sandwich tin comes out?

Square cake tin

Ramekin

Lemon juicer

Sandwich cake tin

Glass jugs

Rolling pin

Oven dish

Cooling rack

Baking parchment

Frying pan

Saucepan with lid

Saucepans in different sizes

Stock pot

Milk pan

Do you have all of these tools in your kitchen?

How to cook eggs

Eggs are perfect for breakfast as they're packed with goodness to start your day. You can try cooking eggs in different ways to vary your breakfast.

Scrambled eggs with bacon

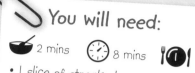

You will need:

🥣 2 mins   🕐 8 mins   🍴

- 1 slice of streaky bacon
- 1 tbsp milk
- 1 egg
- a small knob of butter
- pinch of dried basil
- 1 slice of buttered toast

1. Ask an adult to grill the bacon. When it's cooked use a knife and fork to cut it up into small pieces.

2. Whisk together the milk and egg until creamy.

You can use brown or white toasted bread.

3. Melt the butter in a frying pan on a medium heat and add the egg and milk mixture. Stir often until the eggs are just cooked, but still creamy. Mix in the grilled bacon pieces.

Serve your scrambled eggs and bacon on toast with basil sprinkled over.

Boiled eggs

You will need:

🥣 2 mins ⏱ 4-8 mins 🍴🍽

- 1 egg
- 1 piece of buttered toast, sliced

How do you like your boiled egg? Look at the options below and decide how long to cook your egg for. Fill a small saucepan with water and lower one egg into it. Ask an adult to boil the water. When the water has boiled, lower the temperature and let it simmer.

SOFT BOILED
Cook for four minutes. This egg will have a soft, runny yolk - perfect for dipping your slices of toast into!

MEDIUM BOILED
Cook for six minutes. The egg yolk will be medium-firm.

HARD BOILED
Cook for eight minutes. The yolk will be really firm.

Fried eggs

1. Ask an adult to heat the oil in a pan over a medium heat.

2. Crack the egg into a bowl. If any of the shell falls into the bowl scoop it out using a spoon. Gently tip the egg into the frying pan.

3. The egg needs to be fried for about two minutes on a medium heat. If you like your egg well-done, it needs to be cooked on both sides.

4. Serve the fried egg on a slice of toast. Season with black pepper.

You will need:

🥣 1 min ⏱ 2-4 mins 🍴🍽

- 1 tsp sunflower oil
- 1 egg
- 1 slice of buttered toast
- ground black pepper, to season

Pancakes

Pancakes can be thick or thin depending on the ingredients you use to make them. Have fun trying out both types of pancake. Thin pancakes are often called "crêpes". Make this dish for your family.

Thick pancakes

You will need:

 5 mins 12-15 mins  4

- 1 egg
- 110g (3¾ oz) self-raising flour
- 1 tsp bicarbonate of soda
- 150ml (5fl oz) milk
- sunflower oil for frying
- 200g (7oz) fresh strawberries, hulled and sliced
- 4 tbsp plain yogurt

1) Put the egg, flour, bicarbonate of soda, and milk into a bowl. Whisk up the mixture until it's smooth.

2) Ask an adult to heat a tablespoon of sunflower oil in a frying pan. Use a large spoon to carefully pour the pancake mixture into the pan.

Crêpes

To make crêpes you need to mix together the following ingredients and cook the mixture in a non-stick frying pan on a medium heat.

You will need:

 5 mins  10 mins 3

- 110g (3¾ oz) plain flour
- 1 large egg
- 280ml (9fl oz) milk
- serve with 1 sliced banana and chocolate sauce or lemon juice and sugar

Can you flip your crêpe over? Be careful!

3) Fry the pancake until it is golden brown on the bottom and bubbling on the top. Flip the pancake over and fry it on the other side until golden brown.

4 Serve your pancakes with strawberries and plain yogurt.

Try out other berries on your pancakes.

Why???

Why are thick pancakes full of air bubbles? Baking powder and bicarbonate of soda act as raising agents. They react with the other ingredients and release a gas called carbon dioxide that causes the batter to rise and fill with bubbles.

You will need:

🥣 6 mins   🕐 10 mins   🍴🍽 4

- 4 large eggs
- 240ml (8fl oz) milk
- ¼ tsp ground cinnamon
- 4 slices thick white bread, cut into triangles
- 2 tbsp sunflower oil
- 100g (3½oz) blueberries
- maple syrup, to serve

Eggy bread

Eggy bread is popular around the world. In Spain and Brazil it's an Easter dessert, in Portugal it's eaten at Christmas time. This dish can be eaten as a savoury or sweet meal. Try making it for your family.

2) Pour the mixture into a shallow dish. Soak the bread triangles in the mixture. Only soak the triangles for 20 seconds on each side as you don't want them to get too soggy!

1) Crack the eggs into a mixing bowl. Add the milk and cinnamon and whisk together.

Which topping do you like best?

3) Heat half a tablespoon of the oil in a frying pan on a low heat. Carefully place two triangles in the pan.

4) Fry the triangles on both sides until they turn golden. Repeat steps 3 and 4 for the remaining triangles.

5) Serve the eggy bread with blueberries and maple syrup or try it with butter and jam.

Why???

Why use oil for frying? The hot sunflower oil stops eggy bread from sticking to the pan while it's being fried. The oil reduces friction with the pan. Don't let the pan get too hot as the bread will burn!

Fruity cereal

You need a hearty breakfast to keep you going through the morning. This recipe will keep you filled up until lunch time.

You will need:

🥣 5 mins   ⏰ 20 mins   🍴 8

- 2 tbsp sunflower oil
- 6 tbsp golden syrup or runny honey
- 350g (12oz) rolled oats
- 115g (4oz) hazelnuts
- 60g (2oz) pumpkin seeds
- 115g (4oz) dried banana chips, broken into small pieces
- 115g (4oz) raisins
- milk or plain yoghurt to serve

(1) Ask an adult to preheat the oven to 200°C (400°F/Gas 6). Melt the oil and golden syrup or honey in a saucepan over a low heat.

(2) Pour the golden syrup and oil mixture into a large bowl with the oats, hazelnuts, and pumpkin seeds.

Try using other dried fruits, such as apricots.

Why???

Why does the cereal turn golden brown when it's baked? When the cereal is baked in an oven at a high temperature the sugar in it reacts to the heat and caramelizes, turning the outside edges to a yummy golden brown colour.

(3) Place the mixture onto a baking tray, spread it out, and cook in the oven for 10 minutes or until the cereal turns a golden brown colour.

(4) Let the oat mixture cool down and then tip it into a bowl. Add the dried banana chips and raisins to the mixture and stir well.

14

Store your cereal in an airtight container and have it for breakfast a few times over a couple of weeks. Don't keep it to yourself! Let your family and friends try it too.

5 Serve your cereal in a bowl with milk or a spoonful of plain yogurt.

Muesli breakfast bars

Cereal bars are perfect for breakfast or as a snack later on in the day. Once you've mastered this recipe, you can try it out using other dried fruit and nuts. This recipe makes 12 yummy bars.

> Make sure the nuts are chopped well.

You will need:

 15 mins   30 mins 12

- 115g (4oz) unsalted butter
- 100g (3½oz) light brown sugar
- 115g (4oz) golden syrup or runny honey
- 300g (10 oz) rolled oats
- 100g (3½oz) raisins
- 50g (1¾oz) mixed nuts, chopped

Special equipment: 30 x 23 x 4cm (12 x 9 x 1½in) baking tin

! **1** Ask an adult to preheat the oven to 150°C (300°F/Gas 2) and grease your baking tin.

2 Ask an adult to melt the butter, sugar, and golden syrup (or runny honey) in a saucepan over a low heat.

3 Mix together the melted ingredients with the rest of the ingredients in a large bowl.

> A masher is useful for flattening the mixture.

Why???

Why do the ingredients stick together? The sugar and golden syrup act like a glue in this recipe. They help the dry ingredients to stick together, making the muesli bars incredibly chewy and sticky!

4 Spread the mixture evenly in the baking tin. Bake for 20–30 minutes (or until golden brown).

5 When the muesli bars are baked cut them into 12 squares. Hold the warm tin with a cloth. Take the squares out when they're cold.

Fruit smoothies

Smoothies are fun to make and drink! You can create lots of variations by using different fruit or by adding rolled oats to make your drink a bit thicker.

You will need:

 7 mins  3

- 120ml (4fl oz) smooth orange juice
- 120ml (4fl oz) milk
- 120ml (4fl oz) plain yogurt
- 150g (5½oz) blueberries
- 150g (5½oz) strawberries, hulled
- 3 tbsp rolled oats
- ½ tsp vanilla extract (optional)

Special equipment

- blender

Blueberry, orange, and strawberry smoothie

If your smoothie is too thick you can add water.

Don't forget to put the lid on the blender!

Drink straight away or you'll need to stir your smoothie as it will thicken and it can separate.

1. Put all the ingredients into a blender and run it on a medium to high speed until everything is well mixed and smooth.

2. Pour the smoothie into three glasses and serve it to your family or friends.

🥣 7 mins 🍴③

For the banana and mango smoothie:

- 175ml (6fl oz) milk
- 120ml (4fl oz) plain yogurt
- 2 small bananas, sliced
- 1 small mango, peeled and roughly chopped

🥣 7 mins 🍴③

For the peach and berry smoothie:

- 120ml (4fl oz) milk
- 120ml (4fl oz) plain yogurt
- 2 peaches, sliced
- 75g (2½oz) raspberries
- 75g (2½oz) strawberries, hulled
- 1 tbsp rolled oats

After you've tried these smoothies, you can make up one of your own! Experiment with different flavours and textures.

Banana and mango smoothie

Peach and berry smoothie

Why???

Why do fruit smoothies taste so sweet? Fruit is high in natural sugars so when mixed with yoghurt and milk they add natural sweetness. The smoothies will be sweeter if you use ripe fruit.

Why do smoothies have bubbles in the drink and on the surface? When you whiz the smoothie in a blender it mixes air with the ingredients, forming tiny air bubbles throughout the drink.

Pea and mint soup

This soup can be eaten hot or cold so you can have it all year round! For a different flavour you can add bacon and crème fraiche.

Either heat it up in a pan or chill it in the fridge.

You will need:

 10 mins   5 mins   🍴4

- 250g (9oz) frozen peas, such as petit pois
- 450ml (15fl oz) hot vegetable stock
- pinch of freshly grated nutmeg
- handful of fresh mint leaves, roughly chopped or 1 tbsp of dried mint
- a few fresh thyme stalks, leaves picked (optional)
- ground black pepper
- 4 slices of crusty bread, to serve

Special equipment
- electric blender

1. Put the peas in a bowl, then pour over boiling water, cover and leave to stand for about five minutes. Tip into a colander over a sink to drain off the water.

2. Using a blender, whiz the peas, stock, nutmeg, and herbs until smooth and combined. Add more stock if the soup is too thick. Season well with black pepper.

Extras

You can add one tablespoon of crème fraiche to each portion of soup to make it nice and creamy. If you like streaky bacon then ask an adult to grill four slices. Cut up a slice for each cup of soup. The combination is delicious!

Why???

Why can this soup be eaten hot or cold? Most dishes need to be served either hot or cold, but this soup can be eaten either way. As the peas are cooked in the hot water in the first step, they can be cooled down to eat or heated up.

You will need:

10 mins   15 mins   15

SWEET DOUGH
- 100g (3½oz) butter, at room temperature
- 1 egg
- 125 g (4½oz) caster sugar
- ½ tsp vanilla extract
- 150g (5½oz) self-raising flour

SAVOURY DOUGH
- 100g (3½oz) butter, at room temperature
- 1 egg
- 150g (5½oz) self-raising flour

Special equipment:
- electric hand whisk

First decide whether to try sweet or savoury dough. Then choose the extra yummy ingredients you'll add.

(1) Preheat the oven to 180°C (350°F/Gas 4). Line two trays with baking parchment.

(2) In a bowl, use an electric whisk to whisk the butter and egg together (add the sugar and vanilla if you're making a sweet dough).

(3) Work in the flour with a spoon until the mixture forms a soft dough, then mix in your additional ingredients (see below).

(4) Roll the dough into about 15 balls and place on the baking trays, leaving space around each ball. Flatten the balls slightly and bake in the oven for 15 minutes or until golden.

Transfer the cookies to a wire rack to cool.

Cookie variations
Now choose from the following options.

Sweet cookies

Traditional chocolate
75g (2½oz) dark or milk chocolate, broken into small pieces

Raisin spice
75g (2½oz) raisins
¼ tsp mixed spice

Apricots and cinnamon
75g (2½oz) dried apricots, finely chopped
¼ tsp ground cinnamon

Cocoa and white chocolate
1 tbsp cocoa powder
75g (2½oz) white chocolate, broken into small pieces

Savoury cookies

Parmesan and pumpkin seed
50g (1¾ oz) fresh Parmesan, grated
30g (1 oz) pumpkin seeds
3 tbsp water

Cheddar cheese and rosemary
50g (1¾ oz) Cheddar cheese, grated
1 tbsp sesame seeds
1 tbsp fresh rosemary
3 tbsp water

Pesto, tomato, and olive
50g (1¾ oz) sundried tomatoes, finely chopped
1 tbsp green pesto
30g (1oz) black olives, finely chopped
3 tbsp water

Tomato puree and pine nuts
50g (1¾ oz) pine nuts
1 tbsp tomato puree
1 tsp poppy seeds
3 tbsp water

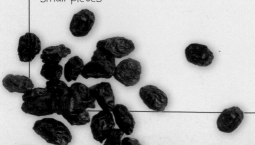

Cheddar cheese and rosemary

Traditional chocolate

Raisin spice

Apricots and cinnamon

Parmesan and pumpkin seed

Pesto, tomato, and olive

Tomato puree and pine nuts

Traditional chocolate

Cheddar cheese and rosemary

Parmesan and pumpkin seed

Pesto, tomato, and olive

Cocoa and white chocolate

You will need:

 25 mins   15 mins   4

For the marinade:
- juice of 1 lemon
- juice of 1 lime
- 2 tbsp soy sauce (reduced salt)
- 1 garlic clove, crushed or finely chopped
- 1 tsp light brown sugar

For the kebabs:
- ½ a red pepper
- ½ yellow pepper
- 1 small courgette
- ½ red onion
- 8 cherry tomatoes
- 150g (5½oz) cooked peeled king prawns
- salad to serve, optional

Special equipment:
- 4 kebab skewers
- rectangle dish that will fit the length of the skewers

Try out this filling and healthy dish. It's fun to create and tastes delicious. If you don't like fish you can use chicken instead.

1. Make the marinade by mixing the ingredients together in a jug. Carefully cut the peppers and red onions into chunks.

2. Slice the courgette.

3. Thread the vegetables and prawns onto the skewers. Place the kebabs into a rectangle dish.

4. Pour the marinade over the kebabs. Put the kebabs into the fridge for an hour. Turn them over after 30 minutes.

5. Ask an adult to grill the kebabs for 15 minutes. Baste the prawns every five minutes with the marinade (discard any leftover marinade).

Why???

Why are cooked prawns pink? When prawns are cooked they change from a white-grey colour because a pigment becomes visible.

Why do you need to baste the prawns while they're being grilled? Grilling the prawns dries them out so you need to add moisture to them while they cook.

Rice balls

This is a fun and easy snack to make. It also works well as a starter for a main meal. The soft rice and melted mozzarella are yummy and have a great texture.

You will need:

 30 mins · 5 mins · 4

- 225g (8oz) cold cooked Arborio or other risotto rice
- ground black pepper
- 1 ball of buffalo mozzarella, cut into cubes
- 1 egg, beaten
- 2 slices of toast, for breadcrumbs
- olive oil, for deep frying
- salsa dip, to serve
- salad, to serve

1 Generously *season the rice* with *black pepper*. Roll the rice into 12 even-sized *balls*.

2 Push a cube of cheese into the centre of each *ball*, then cover so that the cheese is enclosed.

Be extra careful around hot oil. Ask an adult to do the frying.

Why???

Why does mozzarella cheese melt easily? Not all cheeses melt that well. Halloumi and feta for example don't lose their shape and flow when they're grilled, fried, or baked whereas mozzarella changes from a solid to a more stringy, liquid form when it's heated. Mozzarella is the perfect cheese to use for this yummy dish, but you can also try Cheddar cheese.

3 Roll each ball in the egg and then roll in the breadcrumbs (toast that's been turned into crumbs in a food processor).

4 Ask an adult to deep fry the balls in olive oil over a medium heat for two to three minutes or until golden.

Buy a salsa dip to serve the balls with. You can make this into a light meal by adding vegetables. Try a fresh garden salad with leaves, cherry tomatoes, and cucumber slices.

Hummus

Hummus is a tasty snack made from chickpeas. Your body needs protein and fibre – chickpeas are high in both!

You will need:
 8 mins

- 400g can chickpeas, drained and rinsed
- 2 garlic cloves, crushed
- juice of 1 lemon, plus extra if needed
- 2-3 tbsp tahini
- 2-3 tbsp olive oil
- 1 cucumber, cut into short sticks
- 4 carrots, peeled and sliced into sticks
- 3 celery sticks, cut
- pita bread (optional)

Special equipment:
- blender or food processor

1. Put all the ingredients (apart from the oil) into a blender or food processor and blend until smooth.

2. Gradually add the oil, a little at a time, until the hummus reaches a dipping consistency. Taste, and add some extra lemon juice if you like. Blend again.

Add 1-2 tbsp of water if the hummus is too thick.

3. Serve as a dip with cucumber, carrot, and celery sticks. Alternatively, if you want a more filling snack then serve with slices of pita bread.

Extras

Make the hummus recipe and then add one of the options below. Blend until smooth. They're both delicious alternatives and will add flavour to the hummus.

OPTION 1
- 50g (1½oz) sun-dried tomatoes, drained and rinsed if they come in oil

OPTION 2
- 75g (2½oz) black olives, pitted and rinsed

Popcorn

The smell of popcorn cooking will make your mouth water. It's a delicious treat that can be savoury or sweet.

You will need:

🥣 1 min   🕐 3-4 mins   🍴 6

- 1 tbsp sunflower oil
- 100g (3½oz) popping corn

1. Pour the kernels and oil into a saucepan. Make sure the lid is secure. Ask an adult to heat the pan on a hob.

2. Let the corn pop for a minute. Listen out for when the popping slows down. Ask an adult to shake the pan. Let the remaining corn pop.

3. Pour the popcorn into two large bowls. Make one savoury and one sweet bowl of popcorn by using the options below.

Why???

Why does the corn pop?
When you heat popcorn kernels in oil, the heat makes the moisture in the starchy insides expand as steam. It builds up pressure inside the hard outside skin of the kernel. It eventually explodes and the starch puffs up. The explosion makes a popping sound.

Sweet popcorn

Ask an adult to melt 10g (¼oz) of unsalted butter in a small pan on a low heat. Add ¼ tsp ground cinnamon and ½ tbsp of light brown sugar. Stir until everything is well mixed. Slowly pour the mixture into the popcorn, stirring as you go.

Savoury popcorn

Ask an adult to melt 15g (½oz) of salted butter in a small pan on a low heat. Add ½ tsp of paprika and stir until it's mixed in well with the butter. Slowly pour the mixture into the popcorn, stirring as you go.

Salads

Salads are good for you as they help you to get your five portions of fruit and vegetables a day. These super salads are full of interesting ingredients and they're fun to make.

You will need:

 30 mins

Tomato and couscous salad:

- 4 large tomatoes
- 150ml (5fl oz) tomato juice
- 125g (4½oz) couscous
- 50g (1¾oz) sultanas
- handful of basil leaves, chopped
- handful of flat-leaf parsley, torn (optional)
- ground black pepper

Tomato and couscous salad

1 Slice the tops off the tomatoes and scoop out the insides. Put the seeds and flesh into a bowl with the tomato juice.

2 Pour 150ml (5fl oz) of hot water over the couscous and leave to stand for 10 minutes. Fluff up the grains. Add the tomato mixture.

3 Add the sultanas, basil, and parsley (if using), and mix. Taste, and season with ground black pepper as needed.

Try using roasted red peppers instead of tomatoes.

4 Spoon the mixture into the reserved tomato shells. Any leftover couscous can be served on the side.

Tuna and bean salad

You will need:

🍲 15 mins   🍴4

Tuna and bean salad:

- 125g (4½oz) frozen broad beans
- 400g can tuna in olive oil, drained
- 10 cherry tomatoes, halved
- handful of fresh chives, finely chopped
- ground black pepper
- 12 black olives, pitted
- 1 crisp lettuce such as Cos, leaves separated
- 2-3 spring onions, finely sliced

For the dressing you will need:

- 6 tbsp extra virgin olive oil
- 1 garlic clove, finely chopped
- 2 tbsp lemon juice
- 1-2 tsp Dijon mustard

1 Soak the broad beans in hot water for five minutes, then use a colander to drain. Set aside.

2 To make the dressing, put all the ingredients in a screw-top jar, season with black pepper, cover with the lid, and shake!

3 Put the tuna, tomatoes, and half of the dressing in a bowl. Sprinkle in half of the chives and season with black pepper. Gently mix in the beans and olives.

4 Spoon the tuna mixture on top of the lettuce. Drizzle with the remaining dressing, and sprinkle over the spring onions and remaining chives.

Why???

Why do I shake the salad dressing?
The salad dressing is made with oil and lemon juice. Lemon juice is watery. Oil and water do not mix. Shaking the dressing breaks up the oil into small drops that sit in the lemon juice for a while. The mixture separates again if you leave it.

31

Pizza dough

Invite three friends over to a pizza party at your house. You can have fun making the dough and choosing which toppings to have on your pizza base.

You will need:

 60 mins

This recipe will make perfect pizza dough for 4 thin crust pizzas.
- 500g (1lb 2oz) "00" or strong white flour
- 7g sachet of fast-action dried yeast
- a pinch of salt
- 360ml (12fl oz) warm water
- 4 tbsp olive oil

1. Sift the flour into a bowl and add the yeast and salt. Make a well in the centre, then slowly add the warm water.

2. Mix with a wooden spoon until it comes together and then add the olive oil and continue to mix until it forms a soft dough.

3. Knead firmly using the heel of your hand, folding the dough over as you go. Do this until the dough becomes soft and spongy.

4. Put the dough in a bowl, cover with cling film, and leave in a warm place for 30–40 minutes or until the dough has doubled in size.

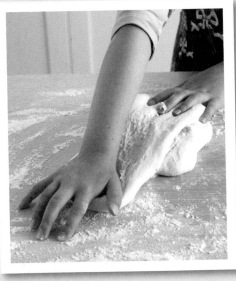

5. Put the dough out on a floured surface, and knead with your knuckles to knock out the air. Fold the dough over and knead again.

6. Divide the dough into four balls ready to make your pizzas (see pages 34–35 for toppings).

Why???

Why do you knead dough?
To create a stretchy dough you need to knead the mixture. This makes the molecules of wheat protein in flour get tangled, making the dough stronger.
Kneading also helps the yeast to make the dough rise.

Pizza toppings

Now you've made the dough, choose from these four options to cover your pizza with. Each of you can try one of the recipes and you can share the end product with your friends.

Use a floured surface so the dough doesn't stick.

You will need:

🥣 15 mins 🕐 10 mins 🍴 4

- 1 tbsp olive oil
- 125g (4½oz) mushrooms, sliced
- all purpose flour, for floured surface
- 1 ball of pizza dough per pizza (see pages 32–33)
- 2-3 tbsp tomato purée or passata
- 150g (5½oz) mozzarella torn into pieces

Mozzarella and mushroom

① Preheat the oven to 240°C (475°F/Gas 9). Place a tray in the oven to get hot.

② Meanwhile, heat the oil in a pan, add the mushrooms, and fry, stirring, over a low heat for two minutes.

③ Roll out the dough on a floured surface. Roll the dough as thinly as you can, rolling away from you and turning it as you go.

④ The pizza base needs to be about 20cm (8in) wide. Spread the tomato sauce over the base and smooth it out evenly.

⑤ Top with mushrooms, then the cheese. Bake for 10 minutes until the crust is golden and the cheese is bubbling.

Why???

Why do you shred or grate mozzarella cheese before it goes on the pizza? By grating cheese or shredding it into small pieces, it increases the surface area that's in contact with the heat source. This reduces the amount of time it takes to melt.

🥣 8 mins 🕐 10 mins 🍴 4

For the pepper and pepperoni pizza:
• 2-3 tbsp tomato purée or passata
• 10 small slices of pepperoni
• half a yellow pepper, sliced
• 150g (5½oz) mozzarella, torn into pieces

Which flavour do you like the best?

🥣 8 mins 🕐 10 mins 🍴 4

For the ham and pineapple pizza:
• 2-3 tbsp tomato purée or passata
• 3 slices of ham, cut into strips
• 1 small can of pineapple pieces, drained
• 150g (5½oz) mozzarella, torn into pieces

Pepper and pepperoni pizza

Ham and pineapple pizza

Mozzarella and mushroom pizza

Tomato and olive pizza

This pizza is made without cheese, but if you really love cheese on your pizza, you can add two handfuls of grated mozzarella before you place the tomatoes and olives.

🥣 8 mins 🕐 10 mins 🍴 4

For the tomato and olive pizza:
• 2-3 tbsp tomato purée or passata
• 3 tomatoes, sliced
• handful of pitted black olives, sliced
• fresh basil leaves, to serve

35

Vegetarian moussaka

Traditional moussaka is made with meat and aubergine, but this vegetarian version is just as good! The pine nuts and cannellini beans give it a brilliant texture.

You will need:

🥣 15 mins   🕐 30 mins   🍴 6

- 1 tbsp olive oil
- 1 onion, finely chopped
- 1 tsp dried mint
- 3 tsp dried oregano
- 400g can cannellini beans, drained and rinsed
- 700g jar passata or 2 x 400g can of chopped tomatoes
- 100g (3½oz) pine nuts
- 250ml (8fl oz) Greek-style yogurt
- 1 egg
- salad, to serve

1 Ask an adult to preheat the oven to 200°C (400°F/Gas 6).

2 Heat the oil in a pan over a low heat. Add the onion and sweat gently until soft. Stir in the mint and one teaspoon of the oregano.

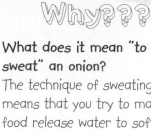

Why???

What does it mean "to sweat" an onion?
The technique of sweating food means that you try to make the food release water to soften it without browning. When you sweat an onion you need to keep a lid on the pan so the evaporated water doesn't escape. Keep the hob on a low heat and let the onion stew in it's own juice for awhile. This will help intensify the flavour.

3 Add the cannellini beans, passata, and pine nuts, and bring to the boil. Reduce the heat and simmer gently until thickened.

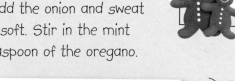

4 Spoon the bean mixture into an ovenproof dish.

5 In a new bowl, mix together the yogurt, egg, and remaining oregano. Spoon the yogurt evenly over the top of the bean mixture. Bake in the oven for 15–20 minutes, until the top is golden and set.

You can serve this dish with a side salad.

Extras
Make a meat version by replacing the beans with 250g (9oz) good-quality beef mince and a small aubergine (sliced). After sweating the onion fry the meat and aubergine until they are well done.

Lamb hotpot

This hotpot is a hearty main meal that will fill you up. The lamb and tomatoes make it juicy and the chickpeas add texture. Serve it with crusty bread rolls.

You will need:

🥣 25 mins 🕐 20 mins 🍴 6

- 175g (6oz) lean lamb (leg or fillet), cut into 2cm (¾in) diced
- ½ tbsp plain flour
- ¼ tsp paprika
- 1½ tbsp olive oil
- ½ large red onion, diced
- 1½ garlic cloves, chopped
- ½ 400g can chickpeas, drained and rinsed
- 400g (14 oz) can chopped tomatoes
- ground black pepper
- 125g (4½oz) baby leaf spinach
- crusty bread rolls, to serve (optional)

① Put the lamb, flour, and paprika into a mixing bowl and combine well so that the lamb is coated.

② Heat the oil in a large pan over a medium heat, add the onions, and cook, stirring often, for five minutes. Add the lamb and cook until browned.

③ Stir in the garlic and chickpeas, and cook for one minute. Add the tomatoes, bring to the boil, then simmer for 15 minutes.

④ Season well with ground black pepper, stir in the spinach, and cook for three minutes.

Why???

Why do you need to cook meat thoroughly? It's really important to cook meat properly *before* you eat it to kill the bacteria that might multiply enough to cause "food poisoning" before it is eaten. You should also store meat correctly and use it by the expiry date. The best place to thaw frozen meat is in a refrigerator.

Mini-burgers

These mini-burgers are hard to beat. Make them for your family and friends. They'll soon be asking you when you're going to make them again!

You will need:

🥣 30 mins 🕐 15 mins 🍴 6

For the burgers:
- 250g (9oz) beef mince
- 50g (1¾ oz) Parmesan cheese, freshly grated
- 30g (1 oz) fresh breadcrumbs
- 1½ tbsp olive oil
- ½ garlic clove, crushed
- 1 tbsp finely chopped onion
- 1 egg
- 1 tsp dried oregano
- olive oil, for frying

The recipe makes 12-16 burgers so you will need the following to serve:
- 16 mini bread rolls
- 2 tomatoes, thinly sliced
- lettuce leaves
- 400g (14 oz) jar of good quality tomato sauce or salsa

(1) Mix all the ingredients for the burgers in a bowl. Use your hands to mix everything well.

(2) Form the mixture into balls about the size of walnuts and then flatten them. Chill the meatballs in the fridge. Wash your hands well.

Add slices of Cheddar cheese to make cheese burgers!

Why???

Why do the breadcrumbs help to hold everything together? Breadcrumbs are dry and absorb moisture from the meat helping it to stick together. You make breadcrumbs by blitzing bread in a food processor until it becomes small crumbs.

(3) Fry the burgers on a medium heat. Make sure the meat is cooked through by putting a fork in and checking the juice is clear.

(4) Carefully cut the rolls in half. Fill each roll with a cooked burger, a tomato slice, a lettuce leaf, and tomato sauce.

You can decorate your mini-burgers before serving them. Make flags out of coloured strips of paper.

Two pasta dishes

These pasta dishes make perfect main meals for you and your family. The tomato pasta is deliciously fresh and quick to make and the beef and mushroom pasta is simple and super-tasty.

Pasta with no-cook tomato sauce

You will need:

 5 mins   10 mins   4

- 5 tomatoes, deseeded and roughly chopped
- 2 garlic cloves, finely chopped
- handful of basil leaves, torn
- 2 tbsp extra virgin olive oil
- ground black pepper
- 200g (7oz) farfalle pasta
- Parmesan cheese, freshly grated, to serve

Sprinkle Parmesan cheese over the pasta.

① Put the tomatoes, garlic, basil, and olive oil in a large bowl and season with black pepper. Stir the mixture together.

② Ask an adult to cook the pasta in a pan of boiling water for 10 minutes. Drain well, then toss with the tomato sauce and serve.

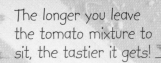

The longer you leave the tomato mixture to sit, the tastier it gets!

Pasta with beef and mushroom sauce

1 Cook the onion in the oil over a low heat. Season with pepper; then stir in the beef and cook, stirring, until no longer pink.

2 Add the mushrooms, oregano, garlic, tomatoes, and tomato puree and stir well. Simmer for 10 minutes, then stir in the pesto.

You will need:

🥣 10 mins ⏰ 25 mins 🍴 4

- 1 small onion, finely chopped
- ½ tbsp olive oil
- ground black pepper
- 250g (9oz) good-quality beef mince
- 100g (3½oz) mushrooms, finely chopped
- pinch of dried oregano
- 1 garlic clove, finely chopped
- 400g (14oz) can of chopped tomatoes, chopped
- 1 tbsp tomato puree
- 1 tsp green pesto
- 200g (7oz) tortiglioni pasta

Tossing pasta with the water it was cooked in helps the sauce to cling better.

3 Meanwhile, ask an adult to cook the pasta in a pan of boiling water. Drain the pasta and toss with the meat sauce and serve.

Why???

Why does pasta go soggy if you overcook it?
When you put hard, uncooked pasta in water and boil it, the pasta goes soft and grows bigger. The pasta soaks up the water, just like a sponge. If you cook the pasta for too long, it ends up going soggy because it has absorbed too much water.

You will need:

🥣 30 mins 🕐 40 mins 🍴6

- 1½ large onions, diced
- 250g (9oz) lean minced beef
- 1 garlic clove, finely chopped
- ½ green chilli, finely chopped
- ¼ tsp chilli powder
- ¼ tsp paprika
- 400g (14oz) can red kidney beans, drained and rinsed
- 1 bay leaf
- 400g (14oz) can chopped tomatoes
- ½ tsp dried oregano
- ground black pepper
- basmati rice, to serve

Chilli con carne

This dish has a kick to it so if you don't like your food too spicy then you should use less of the chilli. You can serve it with tortilla chips, salsa, and guacamole.

Ask an adult to cut up the chilli. It can sting your eyes if you accidentally touch them.

1. Cook the onions and meat for five minutes. Stir in the garlic, chilli, chilli powder, and paprika, and cook for five minutes.

2. Add the kidney beans and bay leaf, fry for two minutes.

3. Add the tomatoes and oregano. Bring to a boil, season with pepper, then simmer on a low heat for 40 minutes, stirring occasionally.

4. Ask an adult to cook the rice using the method on the packaging. Drain using a colander. Take the bay leaf out of the chilli.

Why???

Why is this dish so spicy? When you cook with chillies you add a spicy, hot element to your dish. This is because chillies contain capsaicin, the oil that gives them their heat. There are more than 200 types of chilli and they vary in size, colour and level of heat.

Why do I cry when I chop onions? Onions contain sulphur chemicals that react with oxygen in the air when cut. The chemicals sting your eyes. Your body produces tears to protect your eyes.

You can serve this dish with tortilla chips. It's fun to dip them in your chilli.

Fish and wedges

Fish and chips is a favourite meal around the world. Try making sweet potato wedges instead of chips that normally accompany this dish.

You will need:

🥣 8 mins 🕐 25 mins 🍴4

For the sweet potato wedges:
• 2 large sweet potatoes
• 2 tbsp olive oil
• Special equipment: large baking tray

🥣 20 mins 🕐 10 mins 🍴4

For the battered fish:
• 125g (4¹/₂oz) plain flour
• 1 tsp bicarbonate of soda
• 1 tsp paprika
• 150ml (5fl oz) cold fizzy water
• 250ml (8fl oz) sunflower oil
• 300g (10oz) white fish, such as pollock or haddock, cut into 1cm (¹/₂in) strips

Sweet potato wedges

1. Preheat the oven to 200°C (400°F/Gas 6). Wash the sweet potatoes and carefully slice them into wedges.

2. Place the wedges in an large baking tray and brush olive oil over them. Roast them for 25 minutes or until lightly browned.

To test the oil is hot enough, an adult can drop in a small piece of bread. If it sizzles, it's ready!

Battered fish

1. Put the flour, bicarbonate of soda, paprika, and fizzy water in a mixing bowl, season with black pepper, then whisk until smooth.

2. Ask an adult to heat the sunflower oil in a deep-sided frying pan until it reaches 190°C (375°F). Coat the fish in the batter.

3. Ask an adult to cook the fish until it's golden brown. Remove the fish with a slotted spoon. Drain on kitchen paper.

Why does batter puff up when it's cooked?
Fizzy water and bicarbonate of soda are added to the batter mixture to provide air bubbles. This process is called "aeration". When the batter is fried it puffs up because of the air that's trapped in the mixture, which expands when heated.

Marinated lime chicken

You will need:

🥣 80 mins ⏲ 30 mins 🍴❹

For the marinade:
- juice of 4 limes, plus 1 lime finely sliced
- handful of coriander, finely chopped
- 2 garlic cloves, peeled and finely sliced

Other ingredients:
- 4 skinless chicken breasts
- 2 eggs
- 175g (6oz) of breadcrumbs
- 4 tbsp sunflower oil, for frying (1 tbsp per chicken breast)
- potatoes and beans, to serve

The zingy lime and fresh coriander leaves give this dish a delicious combination of refreshing flavours. Serve with potatoes and your choice of vegetables.

1) Carefully make four small cuts on the top of each chicken breast to help marinate flavour into the meat.

2) Make the marinade by mixing all the ingredients in a bowl. Place the chicken in the marinade. Cover the bowl with cling film and chill for one hour in a refrigerator.

3) Beat the eggs in a bowl and place one piece of chicken in the bowl. Turn the chicken breast so it gets covered in egg.

4) Coat the chicken breast in breadcrumbs. Repeat steps 3 and 4 for each piece of chicken. Discard any remaining marinade.

5) Fry the chicken in oil on a medium heat for 10-15 minutes on each side. Chicken needs to be cooked through with no sign of pink.

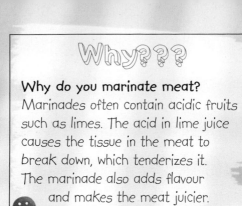

Why???

Why do you marinate meat?
Marinades often contain acidic fruits such as limes. The acid in lime juice causes the tissue in the meat to break down, which tenderizes it. The marinade also adds flavour and makes the meat juicier.

Muffins make a delicious dessert. The blueberries make the muffins extra moist and yummy. They pop while they cook to make great bursts of colour.

You will need:

 15 mins · 20 mins · 12

- 50g (1¾oz) unsalted butter
- 250g (9oz) self-raising flour
- 1 tsp baking powder
- 75g (2½oz) caster sugar
- finely grated zest of 1 lemon (optional)
- 250ml (8fl oz) plain yogurt
- 2 large eggs, lightly beaten
- 250g (9oz) blueberries

Special equipment:

- 12-cup muffin tin and muffin cases

1. Preheat the oven to 200°C (400°F/Gas 6). Line a 12-cup muffin tin with muffin cases.

2. Melt the butter in a pan, set aside. Sift the flour into a bowl, mix in the baking powder, sugar, zest. Make a well in the centre.

3. Mix the yogurt, eggs, and cooled melted butter together in a large jug, then pour into the dry ingredients.

4. Add the blueberries. Mix until just combined, but don't over-mix or the muffins will be heavy.

5. Spoon evenly into the muffin cases and bake for 20 minutes, or until golden and springy. Cool in the tin for five minutes.

Why???

Why do the muffins rise in the oven? By adding baking powder to plain flour or by using self-raising flour you are giving your dish a raising agent. Baking powder reacts with the other ingredients in the recipe releasing bubbles of carbon dioxide. When you cook the muffins the air bubbles get larger and make your muffins rise into a bigger size than when you placed them in the oven.

Extras
Use raspberries in place of
blueberries, or orange zest
instead of the lemon.

Put half the muffins in an
airtight container and place in the
freezer to have at a later date.
The muffins can stay in the
freezer for up to two months.

For the cake:
- 225g (8oz) butter, at room temperature
- 225g (8oz) caster sugar
- 4 large eggs, lightly beaten
- 225g (8oz) self-raising flour
- icing sugar, to dust

For the filling:
- 100ml (3½oz) double cream
- 175g (6oz) strawberries, hulled and sliced

Special equipment:
- 2x20cm (8in) round sandwich tins
- electric hand whisk
- baking parchment

Make this delicious cake for a family party or for a friend's birthday. You'll have lots of fun filling it with strawberries and decorating it with icing sugar.

1. Ask an adult to preheat the oven to 180°C (350°F/Gas 4). Line the tins with baking parchment.

2. Mix the butter and sugar with an electric hand whisk until light and creamy. Whisk in the eggs a little at a time.

3. Sift in the flour and fold it in gently with a metal spoon.

4. Divide the mixture between the tins and bake for 25 minutes. Cool briefly in tins then turn out onto a wire rack to cool.

5. Whisk the cream in a bowl. Put the strawberries and cream on one cake. Place the other cake on top. Dust thickly with icing sugar.

Extras
When strawberries aren't in season (or if you fancy trying something different), try using 175g (6oz) of peaches or apricots from a can. Make sure you drain the peaches or apricots from the juices that they are preserved in.

Why do you sift flour? By sifting flour through a sieve you add air to the mixture, making your cake much lighter. Sifted flour is easier to mix with other ingredients and doesn't have lumps.

Why do you use baking parchment or grease to line the baking tins? You need to line a tin with baking parchment or grease (oil) to stop the mixture from getting stuck to the tin. The oil or parchment creates a barrier which stops the foods forming chemical bonds with the metal of the pan.

Fruity meringues

You will need:

 30 mins   90 mins   6

- 3 large egg whites
- 150g (5½oz) caster sugar
- 75g (2½oz) icing sugar
- ½ tsp ground cinnamon
- 500g (1lb 2oz) packet mixed frozen berries, defrosted
- grated zest of 1 orange
- 300ml (10fl oz) double cream or whipping cream

Special equipment:
- electric hand whisk
- baking parchment

For a special treat make this tower of meringues and fruit. It's a perfect dessert for a party. Invite a group of your friends over to help you make and eat this dish!

1 Ask an adult to preheat the oven to 130°C (250°F/Gas ½). Line a baking tray with baking parchment.

2 Whisk the egg whites until stiff peaks form. Whisk in 100g (3½ oz) of the caster sugar a tablespoonful at a time until stiff.

3 Sift in the icing sugar, and half a teaspoon of cinnamon, and fold them in with a large spoon.

4 Spoon the mixture onto the baking tray in six heaps. Cook for 1½ hours (until crisp). Leave to cool on a wire rack for 30 minutes.

5 Put the frozen berries in a pan with the orange zest and the remaining sugar and cook for one minute or until the juice runs.

Why???

Why do the egg whites go stiff when you whisk them? Egg whites are made up of water and proteins. The proteins are really delicate and when they're whisked they get tangled up. This traps air and forms a stiff white foam – perfect for making meringues. Make sure there isn't any egg yolk or grease in the bowl when you whisk the egg whites, otherwise it won't work.

6 Put the cream in a mixing bowl and whisk with an electric hand whisk until soft peaks form. Make a tower of meringues, cream, and fruit.

Put any leftover pieces of meringue in an airtight container. Use within three days.

55

Lemon and lime cake

You will need:

🥣 15 mins 🕐 60 mins 🍴👤12

- 175g (6oz) butter, at room temperature
- 175g (6oz) caster sugar
- 3 large eggs, lightly beaten
- grated zest of 1 lemon
- grated zest of 1 lime
- 2 tbsp lemon juice
- 175g (6oz) self-raising flour
- 2 tbsp poppy seeds (optional)
- 1 tbsp lime juice
- 100g (3½oz) icing sugar

Special equipment:
- electric whisk

The lemon and lime juice make this cake scrumptiously moist and full of flavour. The runny glacé icing adds an extra sweetness. Share it with your family and friends.

1 Ask an adult to preheat the oven to 180°C (350°F/Gas 4).

2 Using an electric whisk, mix in the butter and caster sugar until light and fluffy. Line the loaf tin with baking parchment.

3 Beat in the eggs a little at a time, then gently fold in the lemon and lime zest, together with one tablespoon of the lemon juice. Sift in the flour, then fold in with the poppy seeds, if using.

4 Transfer to the tin and smooth the top. Bake for one hour, or until golden. Cool in the tin for five minutes, then move to a wire rack.

5 Mix the remaining lemon juice with the lime juice. Sift in the icing sugar and combine to make a runny icing. Spoon it over the cake.

Why???

Why is icing sugar so fine?
Icing sugar is a lot finer than granulated sugar because it has been ground to a powder. That's why it's sometimes called powdered sugar. You aren't able see the sugar crystals in it as it's so fine. It dissolves very easily in liquid which is why it's used for icing on cakes, cookies, and pastries.

Ice cream

Pour, mix, and shake your way through this recipe to make a delicious and refreshing ice cream. This frozen dessert doesn't have to go in the freezer!

You will need:

 12 mins

- ½ tbsp sugar
- 120ml (4fl oz) milk
- 120ml (4fl oz) double cream
- ¼ tsp vanilla extract
- 900g (2lb) ice cubes
- 7 tbsp coarse salt
- mixed berries (optional)

Special equipment:
- 2 resealable bags, 1 bigger than the other

1) Whisk the sugar, milk, double cream, and vanilla in a bowl. Pour the mixture into a resealable bag, close it, and set aside.

3) Put the ice cubes into a large bowl and pour the coarse salt over the ice.

Keep your hands on the towel so they don't freeze!

4) Fill a large resealable bag halfway with ice cubes. Place the sealed bag of cream mixture into the bag of ice.

5) Fill up the rest of the large bag with ice cubes and close it.

6) Wrap the large bag in a towel and shake for 10 minutes or until the cream mixture has become a solid. Serve straight away.

Why do you add the salt to the ice? *Because dissolving the salt absorbs energy from the ice-water mix, lowering the temperature of the liquid to below the melting point of ice, creating an environment in which the cream mixture can freeze.*

You can also serve your ice cream with chocolate sauce or pieces.

Raspberry crème brûlée

This traditional French dessert is fun to make and eat. Crème brûlée means "burnt cream" and it gets its name from the burnt (caramelized) sugar on top.

You will need:

 10 mins    30 mins   6

- 200g (7oz) fresh raspberries
- 4 large egg yolks
- 5 tbsp golden caster sugar
- 560ml (18fl oz) double cream
- 1 tsp vanilla extract

Special equipment:
- 6 ramekins
- electric hand whisk

(1) Divide the raspberries among the ramekins. Whisk the egg yolks and two tablespoons of sugar in a bowl until pale and creamy.

(2) Heat the cream gently (don't boil) for five minutes. Remove from the heat, stir in the vanilla, and allow to cool for five minutes.

(3) Slowly add the warm cream to the egg mixture, whisking constantly. Pour the mixture back into the pan, and cook over a low heat (do not boil) for a couple of minutes, stirring constantly. If overheated, the custard will curdle.

Be careful when pouring the warm custard.

Why???

Why does the sugar get hard and brown? When the crème brûlées are heated under a grill, the sugar on top goes hard and brown because the sugar melts and caramelizes, giving it a delicious nutty flavour. This process is called "pyrolysis".

(4) Pour the custard into the ramekins and allow to cool. Transfer to the refrigerator to set for a couple of hours.

(5) Sprinkle the custards evenly with the remaining sugar. Place under a hot grill until the sugar bubbles and browns.

Extras
Use ripe peaches or sweet cherries instead of the raspberries for an alternative flavour.

Allow the topping to harden for 20 minutes before serving.

Fridge cake

Try out this delicious chocolate treat. It makes quite a few pieces so you can freeze half of them in an airtight container and use within three months.

You will need:

 10 mins   2 mins 🍴 24

- 450g (1lb) digestive biscuits
- 150g (5½oz) butter
- 250g (9oz) dark chocolate, broken into pieces
- 2 tbsp golden syrup
- 50g (1³⁄₄oz) raisins
- 50g (1³⁄₄oz) almonds, chopped

Special equipment:
- 18x18cm (7x7in) tin
- baking parchment

(1) Place the biscuits in a plastic bag and bash them with a rolling pin. Don't break them too finely though.

(2) Stir the butter, chocolate, and syrup in a bowl over a pan of hot water until melted. Remove the pan and bowl from the heat.

(3) Stir in the biscuits, raisins, and almonds. Make sure all the ingredients are mixed really well.

(4) Use a masher to press the mixture into the tin that is lined with baking parchment. Put in the refrigerator to harden.

Don't forget to line your tin with baking parchment.

Why???

Why do you line the tin with baking parchment instead of tin foil? Baking parchment is covered in a non-stick coating so it stops the food from sticking to the pan.

Why do you chill the chocolate biscuit cake? You chill the chocolate cake to make it set. The cool temperature of the refrigerator brings down the temperature of the melted chocolate, making it turn into a solid again.

Index

There are so many fun dishes to try out!

Acknowledgements
Dorling Kindersley would like to thank the children who appeared in the photographs:
Roberto "Barney" Allen, Fiona Lock, Peter Lock, Serena Patel, Christian Rivas-Lastic, Eva Menzie, Ella Menzie, Omid Alavi, George Arnold, and Alexander Whillock.

We would also like to thank Jan Stevens for recipe testing, Lisa Linder for photography, Jennifer Lane for proofreading, Jennifer Murray and Marc Staples for production editorial assistance and Alexander Cox for editorial work on this book.